cloverleaf books™

Money Basics

Shanti Saves Her Money

Shanti's SAVE JAR

Lisa Bullard

illustrated by Christine Schneider

M MILLBROOK PRESS · MINNEAPOLIS

For Caitlin —L.B.
For Emmeline —C.S.

Millbrook Press
A division of Lerner Publishing Group, Inc.
241 First Avenue North
Minneapolis, MN 55401 U.S.A.

Website address: www.lernerbooks.com

Main body text set in Slappy Inline 18/28.
Typeface provided by T26.

Library of Congress Cataloging-in-Publication Data

Bullard, Lisa.
    Shanti saves her money / Lisa Bullard ; illustrated by Christine Schneider.
        p.   cm. — (Cloverleaf books™ — money basics)
    Includes index.
    ISBN 978–1–4677–0765–7 (lib. bdg. : alk. paper)
    ISBN 978–1–4677–1697–0 (eBook)
    1. Finance, Personal—Juvenile literature. I. Schneider, Christine, 1971– illustrator II. Title.
HG179.B8195 2014
332.024—dc23   2012041774

Manufactured in the United States of America
1 – BP – 7/15/13

TABLE OF CONTENTS

Chapter One
Planning for Fun Park

"I can't wait for Fun Park!" I said. "Can I ride the Monster? My friend Sumi rode it two times!"

Dad looked on the computer. "Fun Park tickets are $20.00 per person. Mom and I will have to save money for those. The Monster Ride costs $5.00 extra. How much money do you have, Shanti?"

Shanti's family has four people. Tickets are $20.00 each. How much money does the family need to buy four tickets?

I ran to get my money jars. I get **$2.00** for my allowance each week. I put two quarters into the save jar. The rest goes into the spend jar.

I counted my money. "There's **$1.50** in my spend jar. And **$1.00** in my save jar," I said. "Mom and I took the rest to the bank."

At the bank, Ms. Evans helped me open something called a savings account. She said the bank would keep my money safe. "This way it can't get lost," said Ms. Evans. "And you can't spend it by mistake."

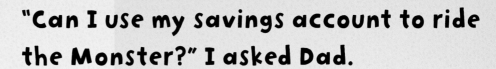

"Can I use my savings account to ride the Monster?" I asked Dad.

"We hope you'll save that for college someday," he said.

Do you save your money?
Where do you keep it?

Dad had an idea. "Why not turn your save jar into a **Monster** jar? Mom and I will save for tickets at the same time."

Two Monster rides would cost **$10.00**. I had **$2.50** from my old save and spend jars. I put **$1.50** into the Monster jar. Then I put **$1.00** back into my spend jar. I needed to have some fun before Fun Park!

Chapter Two

Saving Is Hard

The next day, Mom and I went shopping. "We usually go out to eat on Friday nights," she said. "But Dad is going to make pizza instead. That will help us save money for Fun Park."

Morning Munch $3.50

Yummy Ohs $4.50

Oodles O' Oats $4.25

Fruity Flakes $3.25

SPECIAL! 2 for $1

Pepperoni

Pizza Crust

CHEESE

I had my spend jar money. Great Gumdrops are my favorite candy. They cost **$1.00**. Then I saw Pretty Good Gumdrops. They were only **fifty cents!**

How could you save some money by spending less?

Pretty Good Gumdrops were pretty bad. But I
saved fifty cents. I put it in my Monster jar.
On Sunday, I got my allowance. I put a whole dollar
in the Monster jar. "I've only saved $3.00," I said.

"Saving money is hard," Mom said. "Even for grown-ups. I'll pay you **$1.00** if you help Bansi with his spelling words." That sounded easy. But Bansi wouldn't sit down to study. Still, the Monster jar grew to **$4.00**.

Chapter Three

It's Taking So Long!

Two days later, Dad and I went shopping. I brought three quarters from my spend jar. Then I found another quarter! I was going to save it. Then I saw Great Gumdrops. **Chomp!** All four quarters were gone.

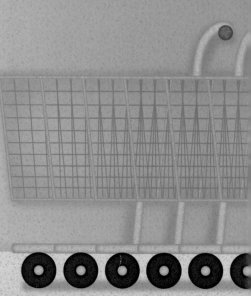

"Let's pick out a DVD at the library," Dad said.
"We'll watch it instead of going to the movies."
I guess there are lots of ways to save money.

The next Sunday, I got another week's allowance. I put a dollar in my Monster jar. The Monster jar grew to **$5.00**. Then Aunt Daya sent me **$4.00**. "Good job saving money," the card said. "Here's some extra help." I had **$9.00** for the Monster ride. **Almost there!**

"Mom," I asked, "Can I help Bansi with his spelling again?" This time, Bansi learned fast. Maybe being upside down helps him spell better. **I had $10.00!** Mom and Dad had saved enough for the tickets too.

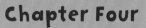

Chapter Four
A Monster Good Time

We had a great time at Fun Park. I've decided to start saving money again. Next time we go, I want to ride the Monster three times!

ENTER

What would you like to save for?

20

THE MONSTER

Make a Special Save Jar

Would you like to save for something special?
You can make a special save jar like Shanti!

What you need:

A clean, dry, empty jar   Crayons or markers
Paper   Tape

What you do:

1) Decide what special thing you would like to save for.

2) Find a picture of the thing you are saving for. The picture should be small enough to fit on your jar. You might draw the picture yourself. Or you could find it on the computer and print it off.

3) Write the amount your special item costs on the picture.

4) Tape the picture onto your jar.

5) Whenever you get money—for your allowance or for doing work or as a gift—put part of the money in your jar.

6) Count your money every few weeks to see how close you are to being able to buy your special item.

GLOSSARY

account: a way for a person to keep money in a bank

allowance: money paid to a person, often a child, on a regular basis

bank: a place to save money or to do other money business

college: a school where students can continue to study after they finish high school

ANSWER KEY

page 5: $80.00

BOOKS

Cleary, Brian P. *A Dollar, a Penny, How Much and How Many?* Minneapolis: Millbrook Press, 2012.
Rhyming text and goofy illustrations introduce U.S. bills and coins.

Cole, Brock. *The Money We'll Save.* New York: Farrar, Straus and Giroux, 2011.
This book tells the story of a family living in New York City in the 1800s. Pa brings home a turkey as part of his plan to save money. Follow along as Pa's plan causes many funny moments.

Larson, Jennifer S. *What Can You Do with Money?: Earning, Spending, and Saving.*
Minneapolis: Lerner Publications Company, 2010.
Check out this book to learn more about how people earn and save money.

Mayer, Mercer. *Little Critter: Just Saving My Money.* New York: HarperCollins, 2010.
Can Little Critter save enough money for a skateboard? Read along in this fun book to find out.

WEBSITES

Kids.gov—Helping Your Family Save Money
http://kids.usa.gov/web_resources/themes/kidsgov/pdfs/Comic_Kids_FINAL.pdf
In this comic, the Cat Family shares some great ideas about how you can help your family save money.

PBS Kids Go!—It's My Life: Money
http://pbskids.org/itsmylife/money/index.html
Check out the Money section of this fun site from PBS. You'll find information on spending, making, and managing money.

LERNER ê SOURCE™
Expand learning beyond the printed book. Download free, complementary educational resources for this book from our website, www.lernersource.com.